MR. NOAH AND THE SECOND FLOOD

MR. NOAH
AND THE
SECOND FLOOD

Sheila Burnford

Illustrated by Michael Foreman

PRAEGER PUBLISHERS
New York • Washington

This book is dedicated to that Ark of today
THE WORLD WILDLIFE FUND*and to all those true descendants of Noah*
who work in every way to keep it afloat, its
passenger list undiminished

BOOKS THAT MATTER
Published in the United States of America in 1973
by Praeger Publishers, Inc.
111 Fourth Avenue, New York, N.Y. 10003

© text Sheila Burnford 1973
© illustrations Michael Foreman 1973

Library of Congress Catalog Card Number: 73-6863

Printed in the United States of America

$\mathcal{M}$r. James Noah lived with his wife and sons in their farmhouse on top of a very high mountain, much as his ancestors had done since the first one had emigrated from Ararat a good many centuries ago. They lived entirely off the land, and the only modern machinery to be found there was a wheel to draw the bucket up the well. Mrs. Noah wove, spun, churned, baked, and looked after the vegetable garden; the three boys tended the flocks upon the mountainside and chopped the wood. Mr. Noah husbanded the land generally, and they all helped with the milking.

All they knew of the world that lay beyond the valleys far below was what they read annually in the twelve issues of *The Farmer's Monthly* to which Mr. Noah subscribed, and a single, rather crumpled, copy of a Sunday newspaper. They found this total content of up-to-date information entirely sufficient. The boys cut out and pasted up the pictures, Mrs. Noah read every word of "Mrs. Farmer's Forum," while Mr. Noah loved underlining the more potent or puzzling items and marveling over things like electric milkers and combine harvesters. He also did the crosswords and enjoyed working out the Brain Teasers as he walked behind his yoke of oxen, or around the treadmill with the donkey to keep it company.

Of course the Noahs maintained the family interest in animals. The mountain had remained a sanctuary to those descendants of the passengers in the first Ark who had chosen to live there as well, and any others passing through made a point of calling on the Family to pay their traditional respects. They were always made welcome and given a hearty meal. Mrs. Noah extracted thorns from hundreds of variegated paws during the course of a year, Mr. Noah was very good with inaccessible ticks, and anyone was welcome to hibernate in the barn, or, if small enough, behind the kitchen stove.

In return, their animal neighbors accorded the Noahs their highest esteem: they brought their children along to be admired as soon as they were able to walk (at the same time admonishing them severely if they so much as turned a paw or hoof in the direction of Mr. Noah's crops and cattle, or Mrs. Noah's vegetables, hens, or washing line). On Covenant Day, the annual holiday celebrated by a truce among all animals, the Family provided a festive picnic supper on the meadow below the farmhouse to which a Lion neighbor and a Lamb from their fold traditionally led the guests. If Covenant Day happened to coincide with the Caribou spring migration, Mrs. Noah's catering resources were sometimes greatly taxed with the additional itinerant guests.

Mr. Noah also supported, with very large donations, innumerable animal sanctuaries around the world. He was able to do this because a farsighted forebear had taken out a patent which applied to the sale of all Noah's Arks; and the royalties, rising to a peak at Christmas, were considerable indeed. All these went to various animal-preservation funds, except for the annual token of a small, but heavy, gold brick. These Mr. Noah liked to receive, even though he had no need of them and simply piled them neatly in a cave at the back door, because they ensured the delivery of the year's reading material and a sheaf of financial statements which he never read but which made good scribbling pads.

Accordingly, on the first Monday of each new year, his Bank Manager toiled the long miles up the mountain, carrying a basket containing the gold brick, thoughtfully wrapped up in yesterday's *Sunday Trumpeter*, the last twelve issues of *The Farmer's Monthly*, a new bank calendar and, invariably, tucked away in a corner, something like a pot of preserves or a geranium cutting from his wife to Mrs. Noah. His was the only other human voice ever heard upon the mountain, for the Noahs had never encouraged visi-

tors in case they disturbed the animals. They bore with him, not entirely for what he brought but because he was a kindly man who kept sugar lumps in his pockets for the donkeys and could be relied upon to find good homes for kittens and puppies in the outside world. However, they were usually quite glad when even he departed with his squeaking basketload and they were able to settle down to another year's peace and quiet.

On the Sunday following the first Monday of the year 1973, Mr. Noah unwrapped the gold brick after dinner, always an agreeable procedure, then, after Mrs. Noah had run an iron over the creases, he settled down to read the *Sunday Trumpeter,* a goose-quill pen in one hand, a ruler in the other. He underlined

busily for a while, and then he totted up the results.

"All the worries in the world begin with 'p' this year," he said. "Last year it was 's.'"

"Fancy that!" said Mrs. Noah dutifully. "You mean that they are troubled with pestilence or psittacosis or . . .?"

"Population, pollution, pesticides, protests, politics, precipitation, permissiveness, plastics, procrastination," read Mr. Noah, sounding like corn popping, "in that order. The picture is pessimistic indeed."

"Phew!" said Mrs. Noah, who always tried very hard to please. "What are plastics?"

"Some form of unsatisfactory breakfast cereal, I expect," said Mr. Noah. He read on, his brows working alarmingly. "Seven billion people by the year 2000," he said, and went to the window, where he swung his telescope around on the world far below. For a fleeting moment the clouds above the valleys cleared and he was able to see the crawling lines of antlike automobiles filling the roads, and the white wakes of motorboats closely woven upon every lake. "I invite you to think of that in terms of motor ownership alone. The prospect is horrible."

"It shouldn't affect us, dear," said Mrs. Noah, "living as we do so far above the world and nothing but a sheep track down." She had to raise her voice as two Jumbo Jets passed one another directly overhead and all the plates on the dresser rattled.

Mr. Noah read on resolutely, "Every exhaust discharges large quantities of carbon dioxide into the atmosphere. The resulting accumulation will form a cloud which will reduce the transfer of surface heat back into space. This must lead to a gradual warming of the earth."

"That will be nice," said Mrs. Noah, who suffered from chilblains during the winter.

"There will be nothing nice about it," said Mr.

Noah severely, "for this will increase precipitation. It will rain and rain, the polar icecaps will melt, and with the glaciers running like rivers in spring the waters of the world must rise accordingly. In short," Mr. Noah went on, barely able to conceal his mounting excitement, "it looks as though we could expect another Flood!"

"Now, dear," said Mrs. Noah, knitting away unmoved, "you know that we were promised no such thing would ever happen again." She looked complacently at the Terms of the Covenant, hanging framed upon the wall. Like all the Noah wives who had ever married into this family of incipient boat-builders, she had always looked upon it as a kind of insurance policy against a maritime destiny.

"The Terms clearly state that a *'rainbow shall be set upon the clouds'* as a reminder, *'in token of the Covenant,'*" said Mr. Noah. "But, if my interpretation is correct, it will not be possible to observe any rainbow at all from the earth once an impenetrable cloud of carbon dioxide lies over it; therefore, I think we must assume that the Covenant would no longer hold water—so to speak—and that another Flood could be justified."

Mrs. Noah was speechless.

"I must start building an Ark right away," said Mr. Noah, bright-eyed, and he ran up to the attic to bring down the roll of papyrus plants that his great-great-many-times-great-grandfather had drawn up to the scale of one finger breadth to the cubit. "There is no time to be lost," he said as he spread the plans upon the table. "The boys and I will start first thing tomorrow. We will build in the meadow below the house so that we may continue to live here until the very last moment. Let me think. We will need gopher-wood, axes, saws; the workbench must be enlarged . . ." Mr. Noah, looking thoroughly fulfilled, hurried away humming "A Life on the Ocean Wave."

Mrs. Noah did not look at all fulfilled. She had lived with model arks all her married life, and knew those plans only too well. At the thought of their reality her heart sank and her feet ached; once all the animals were crammed inside it was always standing room only. And she had yet to see the original depicted without that First Family standing on the deck, foursquare to the wind and rain on a tossing sea, the animals cosily within, only the Giraffes' necks sticking out of the window behind. At the thought of some of the domestic aspects of the voyage ahead, such as housekeeping for a pair of Hippopotamuses or cleaning out the Polecats' quarters, let alone catering to 4,632 assorted tastes and capacities on a voyage of unknown duration, her mind boggled, and her round, plump face looked strained. She remembered reading somewhere that an elephant consumed a ton of food a day. . . . She wished that she liked reptiles more. . . .

Mr. Noah came running in again. "You had better start making a list," he said. "We don't want to forget things like bamboo shoots for the Pandas, a first-aid box, or a basin for the Racoons to wash their food in. And here is the first Mrs. Noah's recipe book, which was in the attic. It should help." Off he tore, to find a stand of gopher trees.

Mrs. Noah leafed through pages on Pemmican,

Biltong, and the Preserving of Ants' Eggs and Frog Spawn, and paused at "Mrs. Noah's Nutritious Nuggets": *Take 20 hundredweight of best cornmeal and lightly stir in 10 gallons of best oil of cods' livers. Shake in, a stone at a time, a hundredweight of raisins. . . . Set the vats to simmer at the back of the cooking trench. . . .* Mrs. Noah bowed her head in brief farewell over her knitting, then squared her shoulders and took up pen and paper to begin her list. "Bamboo, borax, etc., basin . . ." she wrote, then paused for further inspiration. "Umbrella, arch supports, aspirin . . ." she continued.

The months flew by as Mr. Noah and the boys chopped and sawed, planed and hammered, and the frame of the Ark, 300 cubits long, 50 cubits wide, and 30 cubits high, grew upon the meadow. There was always a rapt audience, for the animals came from far and near to see this legendary wonder, and often stood around for days just watching. They were always willing to oblige when Mr. Noah asked them to try out various innovations such as a nonslip deck surface and an exercise wheel. A pair of Ravens built a rather untidy nest on the deck superstructure, and work had to be suspended there until the last of the fledglings was ready to take to the air.

Mrs. Noah picked, pounded, mashed, dried, and pressed. Her list grew longer and longer, and the hillocks of pemmican higher and higher. She extended her washing lines until the mountainside was festooned with strips of biltong pegged out to dry. Like the others she never walked but ran, and never did less than two things at once.

The family were all busy from cockcrow until nightfall—so busy that dust gathered upon the piles of unopened *Farmer's Monthly,* the *Trumpeter* re-

mained wrapped around successive gold bricks, and cobwebs festooned the telescope, for no one had time to do lessons or underline, or even look around—so busy that they hardly noticed when the weeks turned to months, the months to years, and Covenant Days rolled past unremarked, celebrated only by the animals.

Had they ever had a moment to entertain any doubts about what they would do with a landlocked Ark, or even several tons of Nutritious Nuggets, should Mr. Noah's long-range weather forecast prove inaccurate, these would have been dispelled in due course by the reassuring sight of the Bank Manager now pegging up a raincoat to dry alongside the pemmican. Its conservative gabardine folds steaming gently in the sun, which continued to shine on the

mountain so far above the gathering clouds below, and his increasingly gloomy reports of unseasonable weather, rained-out sports events, damp rot, mildew, and waterlogged vegetable marrows, were taken for granted.

It was only when he emerged through the mist one year in an oilskin and sou'wester, blinking as usual in the unaccustomed sunlight, but comparatively unwinded after his ascent, and mentioned his rowboat moored at the bottom of the sheep track, that the Noahs realized the village in the valley must be submerged. But they were all so busy that even as he spoke about recent events in the damp world below, and how the bank had had to be relocated to a higher position for the fifth time, no one stopped what they were doing to listen to him. The meadow continued to ring with the sounds of the boys' planes and saws.

Mrs. Noah went on dehydrating eggs with one hand while she poured his tea with the other. "An Anteater may eat 15,000 termites at a time," she said, not noticing in her abstraction that she was missing the cup and pouring tea over his boots instead.

Mr. Noah stopped hammering nails into the Dromedaries' stall long enough to sign the receipt for the gold brick. He managed to look as though he were listening intently, but, if the Bank Manager only knew, he was really trying to work out whether he could utilize the space between the Elephants' legs, or insist on only very thin Hippopotamuses, if the Duckbill Platypuses considered themselves eligible for the voyage, his ancestor having somehow or other overlooked them in his accommodation plans.

The Bank Manager fell silent eventually and went off shaking his head, so put out that he found the calendar and his wife's pot of black-currant jelly still in his basket when he got back to his boat, and had to toil all the way back up the mountain. It was a rowboat, for the Noahs had never allowed any engine upon their mountain in case it disturbed the animals.

But the year that he arrived and observed how convenient it was to be able to moor the boat to a beaver dam halfway up the mountain, Mr. Noah *did* happen to hear him because he was actually sitting quietly for once. (He was, in fact, fashioning—at Mrs. Noah's thrifty plea—a rope basket large enough to lower such animals as Polar Bears and Hippopotamuses over the side so that they could catch some food for themselves, or have a bath.)

On hearing how the waters had risen, Mr. Noah decided that it was now time to send his three sons far and wide across the world to acquaint all animals of the embarkation plans for Operation Ark II. The Bank Manager very kindly offered the boys a lift on the first stage of their journey in his boat, and while Mrs. Noah was making sandwiches for them in the kitchen, he helped her by stirring forty-odd caldrons of various simmering staples. He promised, too, to bring some eucalyptus leaves for the Koala Bears on his next visit, a blight having hit Mrs. Noah's source, although he was momentarily taken aback when she said that she would need 8 hundredweight.

Mr. Noah gave his sons careful instructions. They must make certain that the elected pair of every species received the message to assemble on the mountain by a given date, when, according to his calculations, there would be just enough mountain sticking out of the water to hold them all. Embarkation would then proceed in orderly alphabetical fashion, and no one, not even the last Zebras and Zorils, need start off on the voyage with wet, chilled feet.

He then sawed the latest gold brick into thirds to cover the boys' travel expenses, and gave each of them a conch shell and a wildlife map of the world that had little alphabetical flags dotted all over it and the reserves and sanctuaries colored red.

As Mr. Noah waved good-by, he suddenly noticed that the boys had grown up, and two even had long beards like himself; so he called out to them to be sure to bring back suitable mates for themselves. Mrs. Noah added that she would very much appreciate an

English umbrella if they could remember that as well.

"Everything depends on us now," Mr. Noah said to his wife when they were alone. "We must redouble our efforts to be ready on time. I think I ought to put some more crossbars on the roof for perches; the fowls of the air will need a rest from time to time. Could you add birdseed to your list? Perhaps some worms too? You could dry those to save space."

Mrs. Noah said nothing for a moment, then suddenly bent and stripped the lichen from the rock on which they had been standing. She threw it high in the air and watched the pieces fall. "Caribou," she said wildly, "herbivorous; two caribou consuming 15 pounds of lichen per day, per capita for, say, one year: $15 \times 2 \times 365 = 10,940$ pounds lichen." She fell silent.

Mr. Noah looked at her doubtfully. "10,950 pounds, surely?" he said, and hurried away to cut poles for the perches before he forgot, even though he was already in the middle of fitting a stout bar halfway up the Wart Hogs' quarters for the Sloths to hang from. (The Coatimundis were to occupy a platform above the Sloths' bar, with the Malaysian Fruit Bats hanging from the roof beam at the top of the tier, and the Trap Door Spiders in a small recess in the roof itself.)

The sons found the outside world quite different from what they had imagined from the pages of *The*

Farmer's Monthly. For one thing, there were no longer any farmers, only manufacturers of synthetic foods, which they found very tasteless after their mother's good home cooking; and it was not every airline booking clerk or bus conductor who would take their gold shavings instead of coins. They had thought, too, that they would be able to trudge from mountaintop to mountaintop across the world, blowing on their conch horns to summon the animals;

instead they found that this was an outmoded method of both communication and travel, and that nowadays there were public address systems and airstrips everywhere, no wilderness or sanctuary without at least one of the latter, and where they ended hovercraft and helicopters took over.

Unfortunately none of these improvements showed on the wildlife maps their father had given them, which was often misleading: Jetting off to one of the red-encircled areas in search of, say, O for Oribi, Oryx, or Orangutan, or G for Gnu, Gerbil or Gopher, they would often arrive and find nothing but an oil field, trailer camp, or food-pill factory, and this wasted a great deal of time.

The attitude of the people, too, seemed very confusing, particularly when the sons sought directions from them. For example, if they asked for the way to the nearest Wolverine, the whereabouts of the handiest Yak, the most accessible Binturong or Boa Constrictor, people either looked totally blank or else gave directions that more often than not ended up at a zoo or even a mental-health unit. They seemed un-

concerned about the rising waters. They said that there were people somewhere doing something about the situation, and in the meantime they all lived in trailers, caravans, or mobile homes and simply drove these to a higher location every few months, where they resumed doing things which they said were their own. The sons thought that it would sound inquisitive if they asked what these were, so never did find out.

As Noahs, the sons were often puzzled at the attitude of some of the animals, which was like nothing they had ever encountered among their neighbors at home. Many of them looked rather dubious, some even looked more than a little threatening, and some quite frankly fled when approached. The sons could only put this down to understandable emotion, perhaps upon hearing that only two of each species could go; or perhaps even a little natural resentment that the human race should be represented on board the Ark in the ratio of three to one (Mr. and Mrs. Noah being discounted as no longer fruitful). But, as they pointed out to the animals, Man alone was the Toolmaker among all the species who lived in the world and would therefore be needed in large numbers to help rebuild it. As for those who remained behind, they would all be, figuratively speaking, out of the same boat as the human species, which was fair enough, and would have to make their own arrangements. The animals, being dumb, had no comment to make on this, of course, although they appeared to be quite relieved to hear that they would be allowed to make their own arrangements.

But usually the very name of Noah was enough to bring even the shiest animal out of hiding, and often when the news of the sons' coming had traveled before them, many animals would journey miles just to greet the present-day bearers of it. Thus the middle son, traveling down the high upper reaches of the Amazon, was able to spread the word as though on a whistle-stop campaign, hailing, as he whizzed by, the groups of animals who had bravely assembled for the day on the marinas, People's Relaxation Parks, or apartment-building Activity Areas on the riverbanks. Sometimes these animal courtesies held him up, as when he found a herd of 234 elderly Wildebeests waiting for him outside Mount Kilimanjaro airport; because they had come such a long way, and looked so hot and tired and bothered, he felt obliged to greet each member personally.

The eldest son similarly encountered a vast assembly of welcoming Rabbits on the Blue Mountains of New South Wales, but dealt with them in groups of ten. Later, scouring Sumatra for Rhinoceroses, he was greatly assisted by meeting en route an orderly little procession consisting of two each of Gibbons, Iguanas, Maned Wolves, and Hyenas, with two Crocodiles bringing up the rear, who had already heard the word from an Armadillo (who had in turn received it from an Agouti via a Stoat who had happened to run into an informed Axolotl), and had joined forces for the long journey to the Ark. He was also helped by a pair of Albatrosses who offered to pass on the word to any other fowls of the air encountered on their wanderings.

The youngest son had a very trying time: Assigned the North American continent, he could hardly find anything on his list except Squirrels, Chipmunks, Porcupines, and Skunks, and had to fall back on zoos, where he soon ran out of gold shavings through bribing keepers to open cages, then hiring helicopters to transport the bewildered inmates to Tibet, where an obliging Lama had offered to point them in the right direction for the last stage of their journey to the Ark.

All three were very good, conscientious boys, who did their best without question all the time, and each of them met and dutifully married a strapping, healthy girl and took her along on his travels by way of a honeymoon so that no time was wasted.

Meanwhile, back at the Ark, their parents were still hard at it; the deck seams were caulked; the hull was pitched within and without and in addition had two coats of red paint, which made it look very gay; a door had been set in the side thereof, and the roof was nearly finished. A lower, a second, and a third story was there also, in accordance with the plans, but with the addition of a chimney at either end, one of which a pair of Storks had already claimed.

The Ark stood solidly in the meadow, with a gangway, broad enough for even the widest animals to enter two by two, leading down from the deck to the buttercups and daisies. A pair of overanxious Tortoises, having miscalculated their speed, had arrived one morning a year early, and were already living on board. Mr. Noah found it impossible to tell which was which, and could only hope for their own eventual satisfaction that they knew themselves. He had managed to bring in a very good harvest, assisted by what he called his "combine": two Elephants who had dropped in one day to pay their traditional respects and stayed to help. Mr. Noah constructed howdahs for their backs, which they self-loaded with oats and corn, later threshing and winnowing by trampling around and blowing with their trunks.

The Elephants helped to load provisions too. Mrs. Noah's list of these was by now several miles long, and it had taken her five years to pick enough blueberries for the Black Bears alone. She no longer looked thin and harassed, however, but as plump and round and vacuously smiling as any wooden carving of the first Mrs. Noah, for something seemed to have happened to her mind, and she could now only produce, like a computer, solved equations when activated by a question. "Lions, dear?" Mr. Noah might ask, and her mouth would open automatically and a stream of essential facts pour forth: "Lions, carnivorous; therefore, $10 \times 2 \times 365 = 7,300$ *pounds of meat.*" "Space required, dear?" Mr. Noah might prod her further, and out would come the answer: "10 pounds meat, dried = 1 cubic cubit; therefore, 7,300 pounds dried meat = *730 cubic cubits of Lions space required.*" "Thank you. Over and out," Mr. Noah would say, and run off with his ruler. It was really very handy.

Fortunately this did not affect her working capacity, as she could always be motivated by her own answers. Thus, when one day she computerized the Shrews, insect eaters, consuming three times their own weight daily, Mr. Noah simply made her an extra large fly swatter and off she went to swat 240 pounds of Shrew fodder, quite happily. Sometimes she was lucky with shortcuts, too, as when she spied a cloud of locusts approaching her scarlet runner beans: Crafty Mrs. Noah was waiting for them and, laying about her with the outsize swatter, in no time at all they were dried, shredded, and adding valuable protein to her Nutritious Nuggets.

The Elephants were very kind to her, often lending a trunk with the heavier vats; and every evening they pressed the piles of biltong into neat, flat bales by sitting on them while they ate their supper. The Tortoises tried to help, too, by foraging for themselves, even though it took them most of the day to get up and down the gangway.

Naturally the Noahs had assumed the habit of being so busy by now that they ran from job to job,

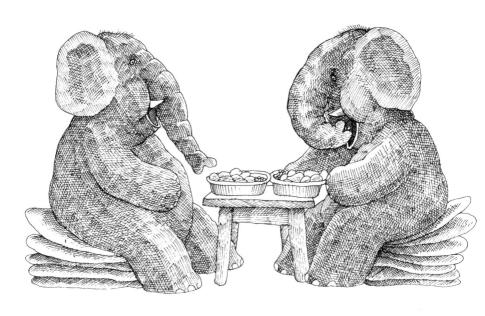

sometimes even eating their meals on the run, and almost as soon as they fell into bed they rolled out again on the other side. Sometimes, if Mr. Noah's mouth was empty of nails, or he had a fist to spare and remembered, he shook it at the stream of Super Jumbo Jets crisscrossing overhead, and shouted "Pestilential Polluters!" But latterly he did not have to waste time and energy, because the Super Jumbo

Jets seemed to be fewer and farther between. He put this down to the fact that they had heard and profited by his message.

It was only when unusually large numbers of Beavers paid brief visits, taking a momentary respite from their monumental task of damming the waters of the world, that he realized that D-Day for Operation Embarkation must be drawing close, and that it was high time his sons returned. This was confirmed when the Bank Manager put in his annual appearance, arriving this time by balloon.

He was accompanied, moreover, by the three sons, their wives, and two Ring-tailed Lemurs, having offered the little party a lift, in his usual kindly fashion, when he spied them walking along a mountain range.

This would be his last visit, alas, he said, as his office would soon be moving to its new location under the Lunar Colonization Scheme—somewhere near the crater Tycho, he thought. Seeing that Mr. Noah looked puzzled, he explained once more what he had been trying to explain for the last two years if only anyone in the Family would listen. The world was being abandoned: A project similar to Mr. Noah's, but on a human scale of course, was already in action. A rocket base had been established on Mount Everest, a computer had selected the best pairs of every possible combination of genes from every human race and occupation, and two by two these selections were entering the thousand-seater spacecraft that left daily at 21:05 hours, nonstop, for the Sea of Tranquility, where a Lunar Government, administered jointly by the Salvation Army, the Red Cross, and the Interna-

tional Union of Teamsters, was already in operation.

The Bank Manager thought that Mr. Noah would be gratified to hear that the scheme had been named "Operation Noah" in recognition of the Family's contribution to conservation. Of course there could be no animals in this New World, he went on, but apparently some colonists were already making pets out of synthetically formed bacteria. It had been estimated that, by the time the last spacecraft took off, there would be no animals (other than those on the Ark)

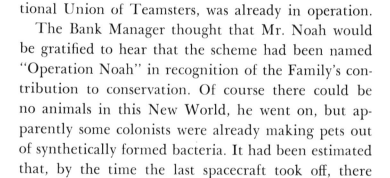

left behind on the world. Apparently they had been seeing to it themselves over the years that their numbers dwindled in proportion to the land left.

He was full of praise for the way in which every detail of the Scheme had been organized: It was flawless, down to the last doughnut and cup of coffee handed out by the Salvation Army before embarkation. In fact, the only unforeseen difficulty had been the problem of the space litter already in orbit. Sometimes the spacecraft were stacked for weeks, awaiting the opportunity to dodge through the rocket cones and other discarded waste of the previous entrants. However, as the tickets were one way only, this would not inconvenience anyone once the last colonist had been landed on the moon.

After the computerized humans had left, it would be a case of first come, first served for the rest of the population, with a Martian alternative. The Bank Manager was certain that the name of Noah would ensure a ticket on the VIP flight if Mr. Noah wished to change his mind and accept a lift out by his balloon?

"For soon you Noahs will be all alone in this world, with only the animals for company," he said. "Will you not find that rather lonely?"

"Thank you, but we never have before," said Mr. Noah. "It will be an interesting challenge to repopulate it in due course, when the waters have receded, with the assistance of my sons and daughters-in-law and my passengers."

"But, when the waters *have* receded, will there not be something of a problem in locating any olive trees —or indeed any trees at all—this time," said the Bank Manager, "as I suggested on my last visit?"

Mr. Noah had been having trouble with the consistency of the pitch on the last visit, and as usual had not heard a word the Bank Manager had said, but did not like to hurt his feelings now; so: "Ah, *that*," he said cheerfully, "that will all resolve itself: After all, the highest mountains will show through first, so there will be excellent drainage, and things will soon dry off everywhere. Our Doves should experience no difficulty."

"Then *bon voyage* to the Ark and all who sail with you, Mr. Noah," said the Bank Manager rather dubiously, and rummaging around in the gondola he found the basket containing one last gold brick, the remains of a jelly roll from his wife, and a bank calendar with the new address and twelve lunar views. Finally he produced two very sticky Bush Babies who had apparently mistaken his mountain for the Noahs' and whom he had found on his doorstep last week. It was they who had been at the jelly roll.

Then the sons and their wives and the Ring-tailed

Lemurs climbed out. The Bank Manager pulled in the anchor, the balloon ascended, and he floated swiftly away, waving as he went. Mr. Noah added the gold brick to all the other ones now stacked in the Ark. They made excellent ballast. The sons said that England had been sold out of umbrellas for some years now, so that they had been unable to bring one for Mrs. Noah but had brought her a nice embroidered apron instead.

After Mr. Noah had embraced his sons and he had been introduced to their wives, he speedily put them all to work. The two elder wives did not like this very much. They had had a long journey and were tired; one of the Bush Babies had been sick in the balloon; and they didn't see why the Ring-tailed Lemurs should loll around eating bananas while *they* worked. They thought Mrs. Noah rather odd, too, and didn't want to become like her, just for the sake of a lot of animals. All she had said when introduced was "Daughters-in-law, omnivorous: $2,000 \times 3 \times 365 = 2,190,000 \ calories$," and went right on filling up sacks labeled ANTEATER from the mile-long stream of soldier ants she had managed to divert into her preserving pan the day before.

But the youngest daughter-in-law, who was an Eskimo, went off without complaint to package the mushrooms that had been drying by the ton in the laundry for the eventual nourishment of some of the smaller rodents. She had brought her two pet Lemmings with her, which was a good thing, as everyone else had forgotten all about them. After making a tour of the Ark, during which they saw the stacks of nice, shiny ballast, the other two became more resigned and rolled up their sleeves as well.

With the extra hands everything was ready in good time, which was just as well, as a steady drizzle had now set in. On the evening of Embarkation Day the Ark was packed from stem to gudgeon with provisions, and Mr. Noah had painted pictures of the animals above their quarters so that they could find them easily when they came aboard. The reptiles, who had been finding it very cold at this altitude, came aboard the night before and burrowed thankfully into the bales of hay in the forward hold, much to Mrs. Noah's relief. The Dormice and a pair of footsore Hedgehogs had been hibernating there for some time already.

Most of the Noahs' own animals were also on board. There had been no trouble in selection, for it was a tradition in the Family that they never had more than a pair, with the exception of the cattle and sheep, both of which numbered seven in accordance with the original, permitted passenger list. There had been no embarrassment with their neighbors either, for long ago the animals had decided among themselves on the pair that was to remain, after which they gradually diminished in numbers, having no more children, until finally there were only two of each species left. Some of those were also on board (for naturally they had priority as neighbors), such as the Chamois, who always got overexcited in crowds, and the exhausted Beavers, but most of the others, such as the Wolves, Jackals, Rabbits, and Foxes, were mingling with the newcomers outside, helping to put the more timid ones at ease. The Noahs' Sheep Dogs rounded up strays and kept the lines neat and orderly. Their Cats kept a sharp eye on everything.

When day broke, a long column of animals wound round and round the meadow and down the mountain, waiting patiently while Mr. Noah rummaged around in the tin trunk in the attic for the ancestral passenger list, which was written on papyrus. He stood at the top of the gangway with a megaphone fashioned from a buffalo horn: "Aardvark, Addax, Anoa, Anteater, Armadillo, Aye-aye . . ." he would call through it, or "Baboon, Badger, Bandicoot, Bears, Bison . . ." and each species present would answer according to its wont, then proceed two by two up the gangway, where they were welcomed aboard and ticked off the list.

The animals were all most courteous and helpful to each other, the larger ones watching carefully where they put their feet to avoid treading on the very small ones, and those with antlers and tusks making sure that they did not get in the way. They found their quarters easily and settled in. The Giraffes were particularly pleased with the headroom in theirs, and the nocturnal animals were delighted to find that they had a quiet separate section aft with heavy light-excluding curtains at the windows.

But long before he was halfway through the C's Mr. Noah was becoming increasingly perturbed at the number of names that went unanswered.

He knew, of course, that there were several species on the ancestral list that could be crossed out, and he had not for one minute expected a Giant Sloth or a Saber-toothed Tiger any more than the original Captain Noah had anticipated welcoming a Woolly Mammoth or a Brontosaurus aboard; nor did he believe in Unicorns or Yetis. But the silence that followed name after name today was unnerving. And he knew that it was not a question of those whose names began with the latter letters of the alphabet arriving later to avoid waiting around too long before embarkation, because he had already explained to the Wallabies why they could not enter behind the Kangaroos, however alike they looked, and he remembered seeing a pair of

Yapocks playing around in the puddles with the local Otters several days before.

It was the silence of the great cats as the day wore on that particularly upset him, for he had always admired them and had looked forward to having them as shipmates. "Cheetah, Cougar, Jaguar, Leopard, Lion, Lynx, Ocelot . . ." he had called and called at intervals through his buffalo horn in vain. Then, at last, late in the afternoon, to his "Tiger, Tiger . . ." to his great joy he saw a stripy figure moving up slowly through the column of animals, who parted respectfully to let it through, and at last an old, very shabby Tiger limped into view and stood at the end of the gangway.

"Do come aboard," said Mr. Noah, relieved, but wondering why such a tottery specimen had been sent to represent his race. But the Tiger shook his head and remained at the bottom of the gangway.

"Are you waiting for your wife?" Mr. Noah called, but the Tiger shook his head again and sadly sniffed the buttercups and the daisies. Mr. Noah hurried down.

Unexpectedly, the Tiger was able to speak, though with difficulty, as he had no teeth. He had come from Kernafuli, in Bengal, he said, and as far as he knew he was the only one left, for his wife had fallen to a sporting oil magnate's rifle on the way and was now a rug in the sportsman's yacht. If he hadn't been so undecorative himself he would probably be stretched out there beside her. And no, he had not seen any Ocelot, Lynx, Leopard, or indeed any of his great cat cousins on the way—or for years for that matter. He fully realized, he went on, that he could not take up single space in the Ark, for that would defeat the whole purpose of the Voyage, but if Mr. Noah did not mind he would take his place at the very end of the line in the hope that there might be some lone lady Tiger somewhere in the world who might yet turn up to accompany him?

"But I don't understand at all," said Mr. Noah, totally bewildered by this conversation. "Where is everyone? What happened to all you Tigers of Bengal? Kernafuli was a reserve, was it not? Eight hundred square miles of it, if I remember rightly, for I contributed heavily toward its creation . . ."

"That must have been before I was born," said the Tiger politely, "for even as early as 1963 we were down to 160 square miles, and a racecourse took the last square mile some years ago. My wife and I managed to hold on by shuttling back and forth between a golf course in winter and a ski resort in summer. I expect the other absentees you mentioned weren't quite so lucky."

Mr. Noah was so upset that he couldn't speak, until this reminded him of the Tiger's unusual accomplishment.

"Forgive my curiosity," he said, "but how is it that you are able to speak?"

"*Am* I?" asked the Tiger, looking astounded. "I didn't know I was. Are you sure? How incredible! Could it be my appearance, do you think? Perhaps looks *can* speak . . . ?" He smiled apologetically at his own lame joke. (But perhaps he was right: there can be no other explanation for his unique gift of tongue.) He accepted a bowl of bread and milk from Mrs. Noah, who thought that this would be easy for him to digest, before going off to the end of the line to wait behind the Zebras.

By the end of the day, Mr. Noah was very worried indeed. He was more than halfway down the list, yet the Ark was only a quarter filled; and it did not help to hear his elder daughters-in-law already bickering

about the extra space aboard, the Gorillas' empty cabin being the most coveted.

He decided to walk down the mountain to the end of the column to see how many awaited embarkation, and whether, hopefully, there might be some late arrivals.

It had been many years, not since he started building the Ark, in fact, since he had gone further afield than the meadow behind the farmhouse. There had been no time. And even if there had been, there would have been little to see anyway, for the world below had lain obscured for so long beneath its slowly rising layer of cloud. The waiting animals, headed now by the Langurs and Llamas, stood patiently as ever, the rain dripping off each pair of noses.

On the way he noticed that the Oryx and Reindeer and Springbok and many other animals had festooned around their antlers or horns long trailing strips of the same fascinating transparent stuff that his daughters-in-law kept their hair rollers in—plastic they called it. He recalled that far-off *Sunday Trumpeter* and wondered why the editor had condemned plastic so violently, for provisions wrapped in that instead of Mrs. Noah's woven baskets would have saved a lot of storage space in the Ark. He made a note to grow some when the waters receded.

It must have been easy to grow, for there seemed to be limitless quantities of the stuff, he found as he progressed. Indeed, it blew and swirled and billowed around so much in the evening breeze that he began to find it very irritating, and he had to stop at one point and fight his way out of a particularly clinging shroud labeled "Nu Brite San Kleaners," a language with which he was not a familiar. By the time he had come to the end of the column, the air seemed to be full of plastic, flapping damply against the animals' hind-quarters, and covering the ground so densely that the Zebras, standing in its undulating depths, looked like striped Dachshunds, and only the Tiger's head was visible above its billows. He saw now that the *Trum-peter* had had a point: The smaller animals would have been smothered had not the larger ones lifted them onto their own backs.

Mr. Noah stopped by the Tiger and stared around, dazed. The world looked very changed. The only land left now besides his own very high mountain was a nearby range rising out of flat, black, shiny sea. Ring-ing each last protruding peak, and entirely covering the lower ones, was a strange multicolored strip merging into a vast froth of whiter-than-white foam. It looked rather like a great, quivering pudding, a gigantic prune mousse perhaps, with peaks of me-ringue lavishly decorated with colored sprinkles.

Looking closer, just beyond his feet in fact, he saw that these sprinkles were actually an assortment of flotsam and jetsam pushed ahead of the rising water. But it was not the tidal flotsam and jetsam Mr. Noah remembered from a boyhood visit to the seashore: driftwood, shells, and seaweed, the occasional orange or tide-smoothed chip of willow-pattern plate. Even as he watched, this strange, gaudy collection encroached inch by inexorable inch up the saxifrage and mossphlox of his mountain.

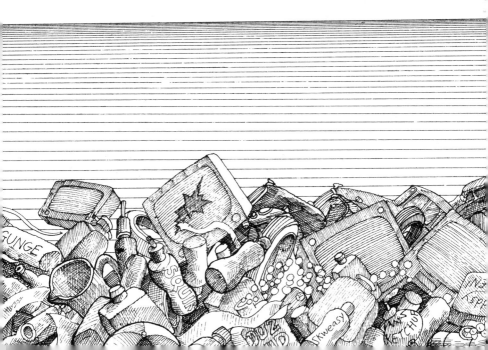

Hypnotized, he watched the heads of some nearby gentians fall before an advancing tide of buoyant and seemingly indestructible curiosities: Pik Nik Kups and Yummi Yogurt cartons, PepsyPop cans and Eggbert boxes jostling the medium, giant, and jumbo-sized shapes of Sunnysuds, Whizzo, Souse, Wow! and other squashily resilient dispensers in the same strange language. Empty containers labeled more simply DDT or KLP followed in their hundreds, statuettes, bunches of flowers molded straight into the pot, brightly painted giant mushrooms and bearded gnomes with fishing rods, chamber pots, and very pink flamingos—the variety was endless. Apparently propelling these upward, and casting credit cards before it like seashells, was the white meringue, a sea of sudsy, foaming waves through whose fluffy billows rose and bobbed the bright, smooth fiber-glassed shapes of automobiles, lawn-mowers, trailers, furniture, and television sets tangled up with plastic-coated barbed wire, tires, boxes, and styrofoam molds of every conceivable shape and size. A twelve-foot hot dog, still outlined by its rim of neon lighting strip, rode the crest like a spent torpedo.

The smell was terrible, for beyond the billowing suds was a solid sludge of dead fish, seals, birds, dugongs, and heaven knows what else, as though the whole earth had spewed forth. Stretched flat and black and calm beyond the sludge was the great expanse of floodwater. It was flat and black and calm, he now saw, because it was entirely covered with oil.

As Mr. Noah gazed, transfixed, upon this scene, a pink plastic bathtub slithered off the upturned oily belly of a whale, skidded over the sludge and shot through the billowing white foam. Out of it stepped two very anxious Zorils; brushing the suds off their whiskers, they picked their way across the gaily heaving rubble and took their place behind the Zebras.

They were the last animals on Mr. Noah's list. He ticked them off automatically. Then, because only their noses were showing, he picked them up and set them on his shoulders. He turned and looked long at what was left of his world and theirs, this putrid pudding of global garbage. Rainbow or no rainbow set upon the clouds, clearly this sort of Flood was not within the Terms of Retribution of any Covenant entered into with his great-great-many-times-great-grandfather: Its solid sludgy source must be ascribed elsewhere.

"Who, then, has done this to our world?" he asked the Zorils, forgetting that they could not speak. The Tiger looked away as though he had not heard, but there was a sudden silence among all the animals beyond, as though they had drawn in their breaths to hear his answer better.

"Who is responsible? What monstrous creature?"

persisted Mr. Noah, addressing the Tiger directly, his brows beetling ominously.

The Tiger looked very embarrassed, and opened and shut his mouth several times before any words came out. "Well, er . . . um, . . ." he mumbled at last. "It appears to have been accomplished, . . . hrrumph . . . so to speak, . . . by the use of, er, well, *tools* of one kind or another, one would tend to think, that is . . ." The Tiger's voice trailed off apologetically.

"Tools?" said Mr. Noah, unable to think of anything upon his workbench that could possibly accomplish what he had seen today. "*Tools . . .?*" Then, even as he spoke, the sad truth slowly dawned upon him. He had always revered his great-great-many-times-great-grandfather, not only as a conservationist and naval architect but as a craftsman, and had considered that he had executed his commission of ensuring that life continue upon the world in a most commendable and sailorly fashion; but it was only too obvious now that he had made one incalculable mistake, and that he alone was ultimately responsible for today's monstrous mess of polluted pottage. However watered down by the centuries, there was enough of Old Testament judgment, wrath, sacrifice, atonement, and other such grimnesses left in Mr. Noah to ensure that the same mistake would not recur through *his* decendants. Any future disturbances to the natural, law-abiding inhabitants of the world would not be at the tool-wielding hands of *his* great-great-many-times-great-grandchildren.

With a dramatic gesture worthy of his forefathers, Mr. Noah raised his hands high above his head, tore up the ancestral passenger list, and threw the pieces to the four evil-smelling winds of heaven.

"I think I had better be pushing off," said the Tiger, diffidently blowing a fragment of papyrus inscribed "Geronuk, Gnu, Grizzly, Goril . . ." off his nose and preparing to enter the vacated bathtub. "No one else will come now. *Bon voyage,* Mr. Noah. It has been a great pleasure to meet your species socially at last, and please thank your wife for the bread and milk."

"Do not go, I beg of you," said Mr. Noah earnestly, "for there will be plenty of room in *this* Ark. In fact you can have the accommodations planned for my sons and their wives, for I find now that I have no option but to sacrifice them."

The Tiger looked shocked. "Ah, *no,* Mr. Noah!" he said. "Surely not *nowadays?* We animals, particularly the Goats, have always considered that a most deplorable custom. Besides, it would mean the end of your species."

"That is exactly what I have in mind," said Mr. Noah.

"Could you not forgive them—let them have another chance?" the Tiger pleaded, his whiskers twitching in his earnestness. "After all, I don't suppose they knew what they were doing, or where it would all lead, when the first one picked up a stick or stone so long ago . . ."

"My mind is made up," said Mr. Noah, settling the Zorils more firmly on his shoulders. "But there will be nothing gory, I promise you. They will simply be sacrificed—denied forever, if you still feel squeamish at the word—of *'the whole company of animals.'*" He had turned as he was speaking, and was striding back to the Ark so fast and furiously that the Zorils had to grab hold of his ears, and his words were blown back in fragments of quotation down the waiting column of animals: *". . . fowls after their kind, and of cattle . . . and of every creeping thing of the earth after his kind . . . and . . ."*

"Poor Man," observed the Tiger to the Zebras when the words finally reached him, and, sighing, he scratched an ear.

Mr. Noah ran up the gangway, seized his buffalo horn, and addressed the animals, asking all those who remained to start embarking right away, as there was no longer any point in waiting. There was no longer any need, either, he added, for the Field Mice to be accommodated in a Kangaroo pouch, or the Agoutis to take up their quarters assigned under the Giraffes' legs, or the Opossums theirs between the Camels' humps, for there was now room for everyone to spread themselves all over the Ark. There was far, far too much room, in fact, and on behalf of the whole human race he apologized for this. He apologized, too, for the garbage and litter they had left behind on their flight from earth. "There will be difficult times ahead," he said. "However, my great-great-many-times-great-grandfather had such a splendid constitution that he lived for 350 years after *his* Flood; so with any luck I may be spared many years to help you clear up and start again. Now, attention, all—and in particular the P's, . . ." he continued briskly, wishing that he had not been so impetuous in tearing up the list. "Panda, Pangolin, Peccary, Porcupine, Polar Bear . . ." But only the Peccaries pattered up the gangway, with the Porcupines waddling along behind, their tails safely tucked in.

Mr. and Mrs. Noah stood on either side of the gangway, disentangling horns and antlers, paws and hooves from Pliofilm Tater Toters and Snap-a-Baggies, vinyl shrouds and plastic lace-stamped tablecloths-with-matching-toaster-covers. Mrs. Noah rubbed all the smaller furry animals dry, and gave everyone a hot drink and an issue of Nutritious Nuggets. The Tiger stood beside her, the bag of Nuggets on his back, still gazing hopefully down the gangway.

When the animals were on board at last, the three sons and their wives, who knew nothing of the recent events, as they had been busy packing up the china in the farmhouse, started to follow, but Mr. Noah drew up the gangway and closed the rail before him with such a doom-filled clank that it echoed all around the remaining peaks and woke the Reptiles sleeping below with a terrible start. His long white beard flowing prophetically in the wind, he raised one hand to command attention. Bun-shaped Mrs. Noah stood beside him, smiling her gentle vacuous smile as always, a pair of homesick Spider Monkeys in her arms.

All the while, as he was disentangling his plasticized passengers, Mr. Noah had prepared in his mind an eloquent, dramatic, and thoroughly long-winded peroration that would fittingly mark this historic occasion. He opened his mouth to launch the initial thunderings, but at that very moment the bemused Reptiles rushed up on deck in such panic-stricken writhings and creepings that by the time he had calmed them down he had forgotten everything but the gist, which was just as well, as everyone was getting very wet and some of the smaller animals were tired out.

"Animals only this time" was all he said. "The passenger list is closed," but so far did he forget himself in his emotion that he took two turns and a half-hitch around a bollard with the Python he had been soothing.

The sons were momentarily taken aback, and wondered what they had done to deserve this change of plans at such an inconveniently late date.

Mr. Noah assured them that it was nothing personal, that they had indeed been the best of sons, and he would miss them greatly; it was just that as a species he was discontinuing the line, for it had proved unsatisfactory. In other words it was time that Homo Sapiens, the Toolmaker, downed tools and became extinct—at least upon the earth. What he did with himself on the moon or Mars was not Mr. Noah's concern, for there would be no other inhabitant there to upset except himself. Synthetic bacteria sounded as though they would be well able to stand up for themselves. He gave his sons a compass, and a map with Mount Everest clearly marked.

The sons accepted their sentence philosophically, as true Noahs brought up never to disturb the animals. They were still privately a little perplexed that their father was so upset about the scenery: They themselves, never having been off the mountain except on their mission, had naturally thought that the world outside was always as Mr. Noah had found it today. However, they bowed their heads unquestioningly to his pronouncement, and hurried down to salvage some fiber-glass flotsam and lash a raft together so that they could sail to the Himalayan launching pad. The youngest daughter-in-law, being an Eskimo, accepted her lot with good grace, too: She took her pet Lemmings out of her jacket pocket and handed them over to Mrs. Noah for safekeeping, then followed to help her husband.

But the other two daughters-in-law were very put out, and thought their treatment offhand to say the least. To be classed as "discontinued" on this world was bad enough, they said crossly, but to be expected to start off again in a new one with nothing but computerized colonists as neighbors—or, worse still, with the unselected rabble on Mars—and without even any visible means of support was adding insult to injury. Only when Mr. Noah said that they could take all the gold ballast with them, and asked the Elephants to help bring it up, did they stop muttering about discrimination and something called Human Rights.

Mr. Noah thought that these must be yet another kind of breakfast cereal, so he asked Mrs. Noah to be sure and put them in with the provisions for the raft.

Just then, who should float by in his balloon, fortuitously as ever, but the kindly, conscientious Bank Manager. He had forgotten to bring Mrs. Noah's order of eucalyptus leaves on his last trip, and now, en route to catch his lunar flight, he had come miles out

of his way to deliver them. No one had the heart to
tell him after all his trouble that there were no Koalas
aboard to eat them. His thoughtful wife had sent her
own silk umbrella to Mrs. Noah, which made everyone very happy.

On hearing that Mr. Noah had sacrificed his sons,
the Bank Manager immediately offered them a lift in
his balloon to Mount Everest. Even at this late date,
he said, it should not be too difficult to get a Special
Selection visa for Lunar Emigration, for who knew
but that they might need a sturdy strain of ark-build-
ers and conservationists up there one day as well, and
who better qualified than the Noah sons? The gold
should help too. They could put it in the vaults of
his new Tycho office.

"All aboard, then, for the New World and Equal
Opportunity!" he said cheerfully, explaining as he
helped load the balloon that this was the slogan they
would find printed on their boarding passes. "Where
every prospect pleases, and only Man is viable . . ."
he added, his merry laugh doing much to dispel the
gloom of parting.

So Mr. Noah gave his sons and their wives his pa-
triarchal blessing and twenty unopened copies of *The
Farmer's Monthly* to read on their long journey; then
they climbed into the gondola. Mrs. Noah smiled
happily and waved her new apron; the Tiger man-

aged a toothless smile, too, and the balloon took off.

But it hardly made any progress, and scarcely rose above the water, for there was too much weight. However, after the Bank Manager, with ashen, professional face, had dropped the ballast overboard, brick by reluctant brick, it gathered speed, and they were soon far on their way.

Mr. and Mrs. Noah stood there, hand in hand, watching the balloon grow smaller and smaller until at last there was nothing more to see; but even then they went on standing and watching. It had been a long time since they had stood still and done nothing, and it felt very strange.

The Giraffes, whose heads were sticking out of the window behind them, bent down and licked the backs of their necks, which was very soothing. It was quiet on the Ark, except for the gentle chewing of many cuds, the squeaking rub of the upward surging flotsam and jetsam, and the soft snores of the nocturnal animals in their cabin immediately below.

The flood was rising fast now: The buttercups and daisies were already covered. The Tiger stopped searching the horizon at last and lay down to lick a paw that had been cut by a sharp credit card.

Hour after hour the Noahs stood there watching as

the land disappeared around them. All the animals within, looking out of the windows at every level, all the monkeys up in the crow's nest, and all the animals on deck watched, too. As the last peak sank under its multicolored, foaming crown, the rain suddenly stopped and, even as they watched, the clouds cleared slowly away to the west and a small watery rainbow appeared. Many of the animals had never seen one before and could not keep their eyes off it.

Mrs. Noah folded her umbrella. Her feet were beginning to ache; she sat down on the deck, and the Tiger considerately moved over so that she could lean against his shoulder. An Elephant's trunk arched over her head and handed her a bun, which she broke in half and shared with him.

As the sun set, the Ark trembled and came to life on the water, then slowly and sluggishly it moved forward, borne on its way at last. Mr. Noah had always thought to celebrate the launching with a bottle of wine, but he didn't feel like it now. There were no attendant nautical affairs to be carried out—no ropes to cast off or anchors to weigh, no navigational course to be plotted—for, apart from the destination's being unknown, the Ark had no steering facilities. Deprived of even a tiller to grasp on this momentous occasion, Mr. Noah sat down beside Mrs. Noah instead and shared the Tiger. His hands were so unused to being idle that he had to twiddle his thumbs to keep them occupied.

They watched the wake of the Ark now, that newly formed miracle of movement that the boat-builder in Mr. Noah had dreamed about for years, their eyes following the changing patterns in the swirling paraphernalia of colorful artifacts. Mrs. Noah's head was nodding, for it had been a long, tiring decade, and presently she fell asleep.

The Chimpanzees climbed down from the crosstrees and joined Mr. Noah on the deck. He smiled indulgently when they tried, unsuccessfully, to imitate his thumb-twiddling, and when they seized the umbrella at either end and had a tug-of-war with it. But his smile turned into an expression of startled dismay when they turned their attention to one of Mrs. Noah's woven hampers labeled PROTEIN stowed nearby: Having poked a hole in the side, they were now probing it with the point of the umbrella, smacking their lips over the withdrawn contents. Not only were they depleting the Anteaters' larder, but that innocent, everyday shape in those competent paws

looked uncomfortably like the very thing that he had denounced so drastically only a few hours ago. Mr. Noah stared at the feast in glum disbelief. But any doubts that he might have had about his imagination's playing tricks were shortly dispelled when the replete Chimpanzees found a use for the other end of the umbrella: Using the handle as a hook, they were now fishing around in the brightly bobbing wake, hauling in a wildly varying catch.

Anyone other than Mr. Noah might well have been tempted to seize the offensive utensil there and then and cast it into the farthermost depths, and its inventors after it—or at least put them into some form of makeshift conveyance to be pushed off with all speed in the general direction of Mount Everest. Such an irritable reaction would have been only human, for after all they *had* made rather a monkey out of him and his sacrificial efforts to shape destiny on their behalf. But he was first and foremost a Noah; it was one thing making global decisions about the future of his own species, but it was not his place to make them for the animals. What was left of the world was theirs now; it was up to them to cast out these furry tool-wielders from their midst if they felt so inclined.

He turned and looked at the assembled ship's company behind him, half expecting to see it surge forward in mass indignation. It stood there unmoved, as though nothing at all had happened—no rumbles of protest, no condemnatory paws or righteous hackles raised. Cuds continued to be chewed as placidly, ears scratched, or coats groomed. Two enormous pink caverns suddenly appearing on the starboard side turned out to be the Hippopotamuses yawning in unison. The Tiger voiced what seemed to be the general opinion:

"Little monkeys," he said, as indulgently as any parent over childish pranks, "always up to something," and he returned with a benevolent flick of his tail a newly landed yellow pail that had rolled down the deck toward him.

So, to the eternal credit of Homo Sapiens, as represented by the last of his species in the world, Mr. James Noah, he did the hardest thing of all for man to do—nothing. He did not interfere. He did not even cry "Stop!" or "Enough's enough" as the unsightly catch piled up. He even managed to suppress a groan of distaste as a plastic Saint Francis of Assisi landed with an oily squelch on his pristine deck, hooked through the bird-feeder screwed to the palm of one outstretched hand. A hundred feet of film, half a lampshade, and a sign that said TRESPASSERS WILL BE PRO followed. There was a lull for a while when the smooth plaster bulk of a Giant Panda clutching a cub presented some difficulty in landing, but this was eventually solved by gaffing it through the coin slot on the top of its appealing head.

Fortunately darkness fell to put an end to the activities. As the Ark rocked on into the night, all the animals, two by two, went below to turn in. Only the Tiger remained, still cushioning the sleeping Mrs. Noah.

Somewhat moodily, Mr. Noah kicked the litter overboard, then fetched a mop and swabbed the deck clean of the last traces before he sat down again. His shoulders drooped a little. He was beginning to find it very lonely and silent being almost extinct.

"Oh, Tiger . . ." he said softly, so as not to disturb the sleeping animals or awaken Mrs. Noah. "Tiger, let us talk . . ." But the Tiger of Bengal was already asleep, his shabby whiskers twitching as he prowled once more in dreams through his dark forest of night.

Mr. Noah closed his own eyes and hoped that he would wake up to find that he had been dreaming, too.

So no one on board the Ark saw the moon come up and go sailing across the sky, for all the world like another Ark.

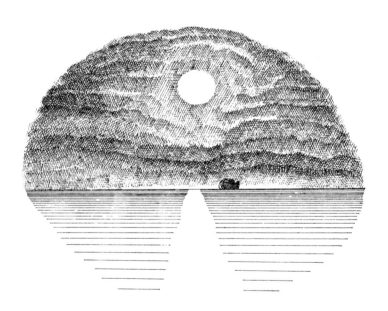